Violence and Disruption in Society

A Study of the Early Buddhist Texts

Elizabeth J. Harris

BUDDHIST PUBLICATION SOCIETY
KANDY   SRI LANKA

Published in 1994

Buddhist Publication Society
P.O. Box 61
54, Sangharaja Mawatha
Kandy, Sri Lanka

ISBN 955-24-0119-4

Originally published in *Dialogue*, New Series Vo. XVII (1990) by The
Ecumenical Institute for Study & Dialogue, 490/5 Havelock Road, Colombo
6, Sri Lanka. Reprinted in the Wheel Series with the consent of the author
and the original publisher.

Typeset at the BPS
Text set in Times

Printed in Sri Lanka by
Karunaratne & Sons Ltd.
Colombo 10

THE WHEEL PUBLICATION NO. 392/393

Contents

Contents

Introduction

At 8.15 a.m. Japanese time, on August 6th 1945, a U.S. plane dropped a bomb named "Little Boy" over the centre of the city of Hiroshima. The total number of people who were killed immediately and in the following months was probably close to 200,000. Some claim that this bomb and the one which fell on Nagasaki ended the war quickly and saved American and Japanese lives—a consequentialist theory to justify horrific violence against innocent civilians. Others say the newly developed weapons had to be tested as a matter of necessity.

Hiroshima and Nagasaki ushered in a new age. Humankind's tendency towards conflict and violence can now wipe out the entire human habitat. The weapon used on Hiroshima had a destructive force of 12.5 kilotons; a contemporary cruise missile has the power of 200 kilotons. All war, violence and conflict at national and international levels in the last quarter of the twentieth century has thus taken on sinister proportions. It is not that human nature has changed but that the resources at our disposal have. No country is free from the threat of nuclear annihilation; no country is free from internal conflict and the barrel of the gun. It is against the urgency of this background that the teachings of Buddhism about violence must be studied and interpreted.

Excerpts such as the following have been extracted and used to sum up the Buddhist attitude to this issue:

> All tremble at violence,
> All fear death;
> Comparing oneself with others
> One should neither kill nor cause others to kill.
>
> Dhp. v. 129

Victory breeds hatred,
The defeated live in pain.
Happily the peaceful live,
Giving up victory and defeat.

Dhp. v. 201

These verses would seem to indicate a clearly defined Buddhist perspective. Yet such text extraction can lead to misrepresentation if not undergirded with a strong supporting framework. Furthermore, if Buddhism has a message for a violent world, it must do more than condemn violence. It must be able to interpret its nature, its roots, its hold on the world and the possibilities for its transformation. It must dialogue with other philosophies and ideologies such as utilitarianism,[1] scientific socialism and the belief in a just or "holy" war. For instance, utilitarianism still lives among those who believe that violence can be justified if more people will benefit than will be hurt, and the consequentialist theory mentioned with reference to Hiroshima is similar to this. Then there are those who hold that certain forms of injustice and exploitation can only be destroyed through violence and that history will justify its legitimacy. The view that violent change is a historical inevitability is close to this. Buddhism must be able to comment on the stance which argues that if Hitler had been assassinated early in his career numerous deaths would have been avoided, or the claim that force is justified against a government which is using violence against its people under the pretext of law. If it cannot, it will stand accused of irrelevance.

In this study, I define violence as that which harms, debases, dehumanizes or brutalizes human beings, animals or the natural world; and the violent person, as one who causes harm in speech or action, either directly or indirectly, or whose mind is filled with such thoughts.[2] The approach will be scriptural, and the resource I use will be the Pali texts. The basic issue I investigate is what this resource says on the subject of violence. Identity is not assumed between the sixth century B.C. and the twentieth century A.D. Rather, the potential of the scriptures of any religion to provide guidelines for action and models for contemporary interpretation is recognized. Hence, the following specific questions will provide the framework for my study:

(1) What different forms of violence do the Buddhist texts show knowledge of?

(2) For what reasons do the texts condemn violence or call it into question?

(3) What do they see to be the roots of violence?

(4) Do the texts give any guidelines for the eradication of violence in the individual or in society?

1

The Forms of Violence

The Buddha's Awareness

The sermons of the Buddha, as they have been handed down to us, are replete with details about the contemporary realities of the times. They reveal much about the social contexts within which the Buddha moved and the faces of society with which he was familiar.

The Cankī Sutta shows a brahmin overlord insisting that the Buddha is equal to him in birth, riches and the knowledge of the Vedas. He continues:

> Indeed, sirs, King Seniya Bimbisāra of Magadha with his wife and children has gone to the recluse Gotama for refuge for life. Indeed, sirs, King Pasenadi of Kosala with his wife and children has gone to the recluse Gotama for refuge for life. Indeed, sirs, the brahmin Pokkharasāti with his wife and children has gone to the recluse Gotama for refuge for life.[3]

Important here is the reference to kings. The texts show clearly that the Buddha had an intimate knowledge of statecraft. Records of his conversations with Pasenadi and Bimbisāra show him speaking in a language which those involved in government could understand. Pasenadi, for instance, comes through as a man torn between his duties as king, involving some degree of ruthlessness, and his concern for spiritual things. At one moment, he is seen preparing a sacrifice in which many animals are to be slaughtered and menials beaten and, at another, speaking seriously with the Buddha about the dangers of wealth, power and evil conduct.[4] What is significant is the level of knowledge shown by the Buddha about the pressures on a king such as Pasenadi. His use of similes and illustrations, for instance, appeals to Pasenadi's experience, including the central concern of all rulers at that time—defence against aggression. At one point Pasenadi asks about the value of gifts and to whom a gift should be given for the gift to bear much fruit. The Buddha replies:

> A gift bears much fruit if given to a virtuous person, not to a vicious person. As to that, sire, I also will ask you a question. Answer it as you think fit. What think you, sire? Suppose that you were at war, and that the contending armies were being mustered. And there were to arrive a noble youth, untrained, unskilled, unpractised, undrilled, timid, trembling, affrighted, one who would run away—would you keep that man? Would such a man be any good to you?[5]

The Buddha thus uses similes from Pasenadi's military world to indicate that virtue does not depend on birth but on qualities of character. In fact, in a number of texts, illustrations drawn from the context of the state, defence and martial arts can be found. Not only does the Buddha make use of military metaphors, but the texts show that he had extensive knowledge of the strategies of war, punishment and political patronage. The Mahādukkhakkhandha Sutta, for instance, uses graphic description to show that war and conflict spring from sensual desires:

> And again, monks, when sense pleasures are the cause ... having taken sword and shield, having girded on bow and quiver, both sides mass for battle and arrows are hurled and knives are hurled and swords are flashing. Those who wound with arrows and wound with knives and decapitate with their swords, these suffer dying then and pain like unto dying....
>
> And again, monks, when sense pleasures are the cause ... having taken sword and shield, having girded on bow and

quiver, they leap on to the newly daubed ramparts, and arrows are hurled and knives are hurled and swords are flashing. Those who wound with arrows and wound with knives and pour boiling cow-dung over them and crush them with the portcullis and decapitate them with their swords, these suffer dying then and pain like unto dying.[6]

In the next part of the sutta, a variety of horrific punishments are described and a keen awareness of their nature is seen:

Kings, having arrested such a one, deal out various punishments: they lash him with whips and they lash him with canes and they lash him with rods, and they cut off his hand ... his foot ... his hand and foot ... his ear ... and they give him the "gruelpot" punishment ... the "shell-tonsure" punishment ... "Rāhu's mouth" ... the "fire-garland" ... the "flaming hand" ... etc.[7]

In another sermon handed down to us, two men are pointed out while the Buddha is talking to a headman, Pāṭaliya. One of them is garlanded and well-groomed; the other is tightly bound, about to lose his head. We are told that the same deed has been committed by both. The difference is that the former has killed the foe of the king and has been rewarded for it, whilst the latter was the king's enemy.[8] Hence it is stressed that the laws of the state are not impartial: they can mete out punishment or patronage according to the wish of the king and his cravings for revenge or security.

It cannot be argued that the Buddha was ignorant of the political realities of his day. He spurned frivolous talk about such things as affairs of state[9] but he was neither indifferent to them nor uninformed. On the contrary, his concern for the human predicament made him acutely aware of the potential for violence within the economic and political forces around him. The political milieu of rival republics and monarchies in northern India forms a backdrop to his teaching, whether the rivalries between the kingdoms of Kosala and Magadha or the struggles of the republics to maintain their traditions and their independence in the face of the rising monarchies.[10]

However, the violence attached to politics and statecraft forms one section only of the picture which emerges from the texts. Violence is detected in the brahminical sacrificial system, in the austerities practised by some wanderers, and in the climate of philosophical dispute among the many *śramaṇa* groupings as well as in the area of social discrimination and the economic order.

Religion, to take this first, is seen as a cause of physical, verbal and mental violence. The violence inflicted through sacrifices is described thus:

> Now at that time a great sacrifice was arranged to be held for the king, the Kosalan Pasenadi. Five hundred bulls, five hundred bullocks and as many heifers, goats and rams were led to the pillar to be sacrificed. And they that were slaves and menials and craftsmen, hectored about by blows and by fear, made the preparations with tearful faces weeping.[11]

In contrast, the *śramaṇa* groupings within this period eschewed sacrifice. Denying the authority of the Vedas and a realm of gods to be manipulated, their emphasis was on renunciation, the gaining of insight and philosophical debate. Nevertheless, a form of violence was present. The austerities practised by some of those who came to the Buddha were worse than any enemy might inflict as punishment. The Buddha himself confessed to having practised them before his enlightenment. In the Mahāsaccaka[12] and the Mahāsīhanāda[13] Suttas there is vivid description of the excesses undertaken. Taken together, the two suttas cover the complete range of contemporary Indian practices, which included nakedness or the wearing of rags, tree-bark fibre, kusa grass, wood shavings or human hair; deprivation of food to the extent of existing on a single fruit or rice grain; self-mortification through lying on thorns or exposing the body to extremes of heat and cold; copying the habits of animals such as walking on all fours or eating similar food. It was the Buddha's view that such practices were a form of violence, although undertaken in the name of religion and truth-seeking.[14]

Undertaken also in the name of truth were verbal battles between different groups of wanderers. The Buddha's followers, in fact, were frequently at the receiving end of an aggressive campaign by other groups to ridicule their beliefs. The description of these incidents gives useful evidence of the prevailing atmosphere.[15] In the Udumbarika Sīhanāda Sutta, Nigrodha the Jain claims:

> Why, householder, if the Samaṇa Gotama were to come into this assembly, with a single question only could we settle him; yea, methinks we could roll him over like an empty pot.[16]

In the Kassapa Sīhanāda Sutta, the Buddha speaks out:

> Now there are, Kassapa, certain recluses and brahmins who are clever, subtle, experienced in controversy, hair splitters, who go about, one would think, breaking into pieces by their wisdom the speculations of their adversaries.[17]

Violence of state and violence in the name of religion were two faces of the Buddha's society. Violence within the economic order was another. The sixth century B.C. in India witnessed urbanization and commercial growth. Sāvatthī, Sāketa, Kosambhi, Benares, Rājagaha and Champā would have been some of the most important centres known to the Buddha, who spent much time in urban environments. As Trevor Ling argues in his study, *The Buddha*,[18] the growth of these cities spawned individualism and competition in response to changing economic patterns and social dislocation. The potentially violent tensions generated are reflected in the Buddha's teachings through such themes as the rightful gaining of wealth, the place of service and work,[19] correct duties towards employees, and the wise choosing of friends. For instance, a Saṁyutta Nikāya text contains a conversation between Rāsiya the Headman and the Buddha. The Buddha speaks out against those who gain wealth by unlawful means, especially with violence.[20] Then, in the

Sigālovāda Sutta, the Buddha outlines rights and duties for the different social relationships in society.[21] An employer is advised to: assign work according to the strength of the employee; supply food and wages; tend workers in sickness; share with them unusual delicacies; grant them leave. The same sutta comments on friendship and says that four foes in the likeness of friends should be avoided: a rapacious person, a man of words not deeds, the flatterer and the fellow-waster.

The study of what the Early Buddhist texts say about violence must be seen against this background of political violence and social change. The empiricism of Early Buddhism also demands this—the Buddha's appeal to what is observed in society as a basis for evaluating the truth of his teachings.[22]

The analysis of historical context calls into question whether any philosophy or thought system can have universal relevance. Since the human situation across the permutations of history is indeed subject to change, the issue is a valid one. Yet there is also a continuity in evolution such that parallels can be drawn between the forces at work in the sixth century B.C. and those operating in the latter part of the twentieth century. The sixth century B.C. is not identical to the twentieth but neither is it completely different. The teaching of Early Buddhism on violence, therefore, should not be used as if there were either identity or utter separateness. In each new context and historical period, there is a need for re-interpretation and re-evaluation. At this point, it is enough to stress that the texts reveal much about Indian society at the time of the Buddha and about the Buddha's own breadth of awareness. It cannot be argued that he had no knowledge of the violence within his own society or that his words were divorced from the tensions around him. On the contrary, their import drew urgency from contemporary observable reality.

The Buddha's Approach to Empirical Questions

Central to Buddhism's approach to the analysis of social phenomena is the doctrine of *paticca samuppāda* or dependent origination, which can be expressed thus:

> When this is, that is; this arising, that arises.
> When this is not, that is not; this ceasing, that ceases.

> *Imasmiṁ sati idaṁ hoti; imass' uppādā idaṁ uppajjati.*
> *Imasmiṁ asati idaṁ na hoti; imassa nirodhā idaṁ nirujjhati.*

Events and tendencies within the material world are interpreted from the standpoint of causality. Phenomena are conditioned. Buddhism, therefore, calls for an analytical attitude in dealing with anything to do with human life, including the question of violence.[23]

One consequence which flows from this is that generalizations and statements based on categories of pure reason are suspect. Evidence can be drawn from the suttas to show that the Buddha insisted on making discriminations when presented with dogmatically held views. For instance, in the Subha Sutta, Subha comes out with the view that a householder is accomplishing the right path and one who has renounced is not. The Buddha replies: "On this point, brahmin youth, I discriminate, on this point I do not speak definitely." He stresses that both householder (*gihin*) and the one who has renounced (*pabbajita*) can be living wrongly; both can be living rightly. The deciding factor is not the label, but rightness of action, speech and thought.[24]

A similar approach can be seen in the Esukārī Sutta where the Buddha speaks about service. In this case, the deciding factor as to whether a person should serve is whether the one who serves is better for the service in terms of such things as growing in moral habit and wisdom.[25] Then, when faced with the question of sacrifice by the brahmin Ujjaya, there is again discrimination according to condition. Not every sacrifice is blameworthy. Where living creatures are not killed or where the sacrifice is an offering for the welfare of the family, there is no blame: "No, brahmin, I do not praise every sacrifice. Yet, I would not withhold praise from every sacrifice."[26] The deciding factor here is the presence of suffering for animals.

Paṭicca samuppāda opposes the human tendency to generalize and encourages analysis on the basis of empirical data and moral values applied to these.[27] It criticizes standpoints which use inappropriate categories through insufficient observation and dogmatic statements about right and wrong which do not take empirically observed facts into account.

To understand Early Buddhism's analysis of violence, this conditionality is important. When the Buddha speaks about the causes and the remedies of violence, his approach is dependent on the conditions prevalent in a particular situation. For instance, psychological factors are not emphasized when the Buddha is speaking to those in power about societal disruption; social and economic causes are stressed instead.[28] Yet, in other contexts, particularly when monks are addressed, it is the psychological factor which is given prominence.[29] In contrast again, with King Pasenadi, the Buddha does not condemn violence in defence of the realm but places it within the larger context of impermanence and death to encourage reflection.[30]

It is possible to hold together the above divergent emphases if we bear in mind the full implications of conditionality and the empiricism of Early Buddhism. We should not expect dogmatic, non-empirical generalizations. For instance, if craving (*tanhā*) is to be posited as the root of much violence, it would not follow that every situation was conditioned by *tanhā* in the same way or that the remedy in each situation would be identical. Likewise, it would not follow that what was incumbent on one type of person in one situation would be incumbent on all sections of society in all contexts.

2

Reasons for Buddhism's Attitude
to Violence

Before looking more closely at what is said about the roots of violence, it is worth drawing out reasons given in the texts for the avoidance, questioning or non-espousal of violence. Interconnected frameworks emerge: *nibbāna* as the goal of the spiritual life; the demands of *mettā* and *karuṇā* (loving kindness and compassion); the need for peace, concord and harmony within society.

Since the ultimate goal of the spiritual path for the Buddhist is *nibbāna,* attitudes towards violence must first be seen in relation to it. *Nibbāna* is the ultimate eradication of *dukkha.* It is a possible goal within this life and, among other things, involves a complete de-toxification of the mind from greed, hatred and delusion, a revolution in the way the world is perceived, freedom from craving and liberation from the delusion of ego. The *Therīgāthā* or Songs of the Sisters contain some of the most moving testimonies to this reality; they are paeons of joy about liberation:

> Mine is the ecstasy of freedom won
> As Path merges in Fruit and Fruit in Path.
> Holding to nought, I in Nibbāna live,
> This five-grouped being have I understood.
> Cut from its root, all onward growth is stayed,
> I too am stayed, victor on basis sure
> Immovable. Rebirth comes never more.[31]

Nibbāna and *saṁsāra* are antithetical. One is the ceasing of the other. In the context of the goal of *nibbāna*, actions, thoughts and words can be evaluated as to whether they build *saṁsāra* or lead to *nibbāna*: whether they are unskilled (*akusala*) or skilled (*kusala*). Indulgence in violence is normally deemed *akusala*. In other words, it cannot lead to the goal of *nibbāna*. In the Ambalaṭṭhika-Rāhulovāda Sutta, the Buddha says to the Venerable Rāhula:

> If you, Rāhula, are desirous of doing a deed with the body, you should reflect on the deed with the body, thus: "That deed which I am desirous of doing with the body is a deed of the body that might conduce to the harm of self and that might conduce to the harm of others and that might conduce to the harm of both; this deed of body is unskilled (*akusala*), its yield is anguish, its result is anguish." [32]

Harm to others is central to what is unskilled. In the Sallekha Sutta advice is given to monks about the cleansing of the mind as the basis of spiritual progress. Foremost among the thoughts which have to be cleansed are those connected with harming and violence; both represent unskilled states which lead downwards:

> Cunda, as every unskilled state leads downwards, as every skilled state leads upwards, even so, Cunda, does non-harming (*avihiṁsā*) come to be a higher state for an individual who is harmful, does restraint from onslaught on creatures come to be a higher state for the individual who makes onslaught on creatures. [33]

When the Buddha is in conversation with Bhaddiya, *sārambha* is added to *lobha, dosa* and *moha* (lust, hatred and delusion) as a defilement which flows from them. *Sārambha* can be translated as "accompanied by violence." As the mind filled with *lobha, dosa* and *moha* is led to actions which are *akusala*, so is the mind filled with the violence which accompanies the triad. All lead to a person's loss:

"Now what think you, Bhaddiya? When freedom from malice (*adosa*) ... from delusion (*amoha*) ... from violence (*asārambha*) that goes with these arises within oneself, does it arise to one's profit or to one's loss?" – "To one's profit, sir."[34]

The point of the above suttas is that violent action and violent thought, actions which harm and debase others and thoughts which contemplate the same, stand in the way of spiritual growth and the self-conquest which leads to the goal of existence. In this respect, indulging in violence is doing to oneself what an enemy would wish. It is a form of self-harming:

> He who is exceedingly corrupt
> like a *maluva* creeper strangling a *sal* tree
> does to himself what an enemy would wish.

Dhp. v. 162

In contrast, abstaining from violence has personal benefit in the present and in the future. It is part of the training of mind and body which lays the foundation for spiritual progress.

The accusation has been made that the application of the terms *kusala* and *akusala* are oriented only towards an individualistic goal, making the motivation for abstention from violence a selfish one. But it can be argued that the distinction between altruism and egoism breaks down for anyone truly following the Noble Eightfold Path. There are also many textual references to the inherent importance of harmony, justice and compassion in society to balance those passages which seem to be solely individualistic. Harmony and justice are recognized as worthwhile in themselves as well as a prerequisite for the spiritual progress of society's members. Hence, in society, violence is to be eschewed because it brings pain to beings with similar feelings to oneself:

> All tremble at violence,
> Life is dear to all.
> Comparing others with oneself
> One should neither kill nor cause others to kill.

Dhp. v. 130

On the level of personal analogy, men and women are to condemn violence. It is an analogy which demands *mettā* (loving kindness) and *karuṇā* (compassion) of the human being.[35] They call on a frame of mind which cannot remain insensitive to suffering in others or untouched by the agony produced by violence. Non-violence, therefore, arises through the urge to prevent anguish in others:

> Comparing oneself with others in such terms as "Just as I am so are they, just as they are so am I" (*yathā ahaṁ tathā ete yathā ete tathā ahaṁ*), one should neither kill nor cause others to kill.

> Snp. v. 705

The Buddha, however, did not credit all people with this level of awareness. He is recorded as saying that shame and fear of blame protect the world, and if there were not these forces, the world would come to confusion and promiscuity.[36] Not all beings rally to the call for compassion on the grounds that others have like feelings to themselves or that harmony in society is necessary. Therefore, some texts invoke the concepts of heaven and hell, rewards and punishments, to control violence. Vivid pictures are drawn of the agonies of hell:

> Brahmin youth, here some woman or man is one who makes onslaught on creatures, is cruel, bloody-handed, intent on injuring and killing, and without mercy to living creatures. Because of that deed, accomplished thus, firmly held thus, he, at breaking up of the body after dying, arises in the sorrowful way, the bad bourn, the Downfall, the Niraya.[37]

> Even so, monks, that anguish and dejection that man experiences while he is being stabbed with three hundred spears, compared with the anguish of Niraya Hell does not count, it does not amount even to an infinitesimal fraction of it, it cannot even be compared to it. Monks, the guardians of Niraya Hell subject him to what is called the fivefold pinion. They drive a red-

hot iron stake through each hand and each foot and a red-hot iron stake through his breast. Thereat, he feels feelings that are painful, sharp and severe. But he does not do his time until he makes an end of that evil deed.[38]

Here, self-interest in terms of avoidance of future pain is appealed to as a reason to desist from violence. This emphasis can also be seen in the Petavatthu in which those fallen to the realm of the *petas* speak to those on the human level about the reasons for their suffering.[39] Falsehood, failing in the duties of wife or husband, stinginess and fraud are some of the actions mentioned. Story No. 32, however, speaks of a deerhunter who explains that he was "a ruthless man of bloody hands": "Among harmless creatures, I, with wicked mind, walked about, very ruthless, ever finding delight in slaying others unrestrained," he declares in verse three. His punishment is to be devoured by dogs during the daytime, the hours when he used to be involved in slaughter. He is able to teach the living that the First Precept should be kept and that it applies not only to the killing of human beings but also to animals. The deerhunter, therefore, is held up as an authoritative witness to what happens to violent individuals. His story is useful as a deterrent to socially disruptive elements and is confirmation of the importance Buddhism places on non-violence within the social fabric. The threat of future punishment is used to control potentially violent elements.

Two broad, interconnected areas, therefore, emerge in the reasons for the condemnation of violence within the Early Buddhist texts. Firstly, thoughts of violence and violent action are defilements and must be eradicated if *nibbāna* is to be reached. In this light, *nibbāna* is the highest ethical good. This stress alone, however, can lead to distortion if *nibbāna* is seen as a metaphysical state above the empirical world and the path to it as divorced from society. Early Buddhism was rooted in the empirical. Violence was to be repudiated because it caused anguish to men and women and disruption in society. The human person was seen as precious. Harming a being who desired happiness and felt pain could rarely be right. If a society was to be established in which people could live without fear and with the freedom of mind to follow the Eightfold Path, violence had to be eschewed.

The question of political, defensive violence, however, must be mentioned here. Can violence be justified in a situation where the state needs to defend its citizens against external and internal threats? Is this a situation in which violence is not condemned? The texts suggest Buddhism would here insist on discrimination. The Cakkavatti Sīhanāda Sutta gives this advice to the righteous king:

> This, dear son, that you, leaning on the Dhamma, honouring, respecting and revering it, doing homage to it, hallowing it, being yourself a Dhamma-banner, a Dhamma-signal, having the Dhamma as your master, should provide the right watch, ward and protection for your own folk, for the army, for the nobles, for vassals and brahmins and householders, for town and country dwellers, for the religious world and for beasts and birds.[40]

This passage implies that the need for an army and consequently for the use of force in defence is accepted as a worldly necessity. But the picture which emerges is not glorification of the "just" war but an appeal for war and violence to be seen against a higher set of values.

Relevant perspectives on these political realities are seen in the Buddha's advice to the Vajjians and to King Pasenadi. The Vajjians are faced with vicious aggression from King Ajātasattu, King of Magadha, who is bent on destroying them. The latter sends a brahmin to the Buddha for advice and a prediction about how successful he will be in war. The very fact that he does so shows that he does not consider the Buddha either ill-informed or dismissive of such political conflicts. The reply he receives is significant. The Buddha does not refer directly to Ajātasattu but implies that the use of arms against a people who are morally pure and in concord would be fruitless. His words to Ajātasattu become words of advice to the Vajjians that they should meet together in concord and give respect to their elders, their ancient institutions, their traditions and their women. No mention is made of the Vajjian military strength; only of their moral strength. Moral strength is held up as defence against violence. Yet it is not denied but implicitly understood that the Vajjians would have to use force to repulse aggression, and also present is an implicit condemnation of Ajātasattu's intentions.[41]

King Pasenadi is also seen in conflict with Ajātasattu, meeting force with force. At first, Ajātasattu is the aggressor and the victor. The reported response of the Buddha is significant:

> Monks, the King of Magadha, Ajātasattu, son of the Vedehi Princess, is a friend to, an intimate of, mixed up with, whatever is evil. The Kosalan King Pasenadi is a friend to, an intimate of, mixed up with, whatever is good.[42]

Thus Pasenadi's role as defender of the nation against aggression is accepted as necessary and praiseworthy. In the next battle, Pasenadi is the victor. Ajātasattu's army is confiscated but Pasenadi is merciful enough to grant Ajātasattu his life. It is still Ajātasattu who is condemned. His fate is seen in kammic terms:

> A man may spoil another just so far
> As it may serve his ends, but when he's spoiled
> By others he, despoiled, spoils yet again.
> So long as evil's fruit is not matured
> The fool does fancy: "Now's the hour, the chance!"
> But when the deed bears fruit, he fareth ill.
> The slayer gets a slayer in his turn,
> The conqueror gets one who conquers him,
> The abuser wins abuse, the annoyer frets:
> Thus by the evolution of the deed
> A man who spoils is spoiled in his turn.[43]

In one respect, Pasenadi becomes an instrument of kamma for Ajātasattu. At another level, acceptance of political realities emerges.

The king has a duty to protect his citizens from external threats of violence. Therefore, the advice given to a king or those with responsibility for government about reacting to the violence of others is fitted to the situation, a situation in which the use of violence may become a political necessity in a world governed by craving (*taṇhā*). Yet, even with affairs of state, war is placed in the perspective of a more important set of values. To Pasenadi, burdened by responsibility, the Buddha says:

> Noble and brahmin, commoner and serf,
> None can evade and play the truant here:
> The impending doom overwhelms one and all.
> Here is no place for strife with elephants
> Or chariots of war or infantry,
> Nay, nor for war or woven spell or curse
> Nor may finance avail to win the day.[44]

War is not presented as worthy of praise in itself. It is recognized that battle cannot take place without hatred and the wish to kill, in both the mind of aggressor and victim. A Saṁyutta Nikāya passage illustrates this. A fighting man comes to the Buddha and explains his belief that the warrior who is killed whilst fighting energetically in battle is reborn in the company of the Devas of Passionate Delight. The Buddha's answer condemns this idea as perverted. A warrior is always led by the idea, "Let those beings be exterminated so that they may be never thought to have existed." Such a view can only lead downwards rather than to any heavenly world. The Buddha thus rejects any glorification of war, since there can be no glory when the mind is dominated by hate.

Another duty of the state is to punish. Punishment, although a harming of creatures and a cause of pain to them, is nevertheless seen as a social necessity because of the need to protect society from the greater violence which would flow from undeterred greed. Fear of punishment (*daṇḍabhaya*) is described in vivid terms, with the mention of specific punishments. A man sees them and thinks: "If I were to do such deeds as those for which the rajahs seize a bandit, a miscreant, and so treat him ... they would surely treat me in like manner."[46] Important here is the fact that Early Buddhism would make discriminations about the question of punishment. As a deterrent, punishment has value. Meted out as an expression of hate, it is to be rejected. Inflicted where social justice is the requisite, it is also condemned, as seen in the Kūṭadanta Sutta, referred to in the next part.

3

The Roots of Violence

The Attadaṇḍa Sutta of the Sutta Nipāta is the voice of someone overcome by despair because of the violence he sees:

> Fear results from resorting to violence—just look at how people quarrel and fight. But let me tell you now of the kind of dismay and terror that I have felt.
>
> Seeing people struggling like fish, writhing in shallow water, with enmity against one another, I became afraid.
>
> At one time, I had wanted to find some place where I could take shelter, but I never saw such a place. There is nothing in this world that is solid at base and not a part of it that is changeless.
>
> I had seen them all trapped in mutual conflict and that is why I had felt so repelled. But then I noticed something buried deep in their hearts. It was—I could just make it out—a dart.[47]

The above is from a translation of the Sutta Nipāta which attempts to preserve the spirit of the text rather than the letter. Here it is the spirit of dismay and fear leading to discovery which is of prime importance. The speaker detects a common root—the dart of craving (*taṇhā*) and greed (*lobha*)—a view directly in line with the Four Noble Truths. Violence arises because the right nourishment is present.

However, it has been pointed out earlier that differences may exist in the way in which *taṇhā* conditions situations of violence. On analysis, two broad and mutually interdependent areas emerge:

(1) violence arising from an individual's maladjustment, and (2) craving and violence arising from unsatisfactory social and environmental conditions, caused by the craving of others.

The latter can be taken first with reference to the following texts: The Kūṭadanta Sutta; the Cakkavatti Sīhanāda Sutta; and certain Aṅguttara Nikāya passages. The first weaves a myth within a myth. The inner myth tells the story of a king, King Wide-Realm, whose land is wracked with discontent and crime such that people are afraid to walk in the streets for fear of violence.

The king's solution is to hold a sacrifice for the nation and he goes to a holy man for advice. But the king is not given what he expects. The sage tells the king that fines, bonds and death for the wrongdoers would be self-defeating. Punishment is not the right path. On the contrary, it would increase the malady because the root causes remained untouched, in this instance, economic injustice and poverty. King Wide-Realm is advised to give food and seed corn to farmers, capital to traders and food to those in government service:

> But perchance his majesty might think: "I'll soon put a stop to these scoundrels' game by degradation and banishment and fines and bonds and death." But their licence cannot be satisfactorily put a stop to so. The remnant left unpunished would still go on harassing the realm. Now there is one method to adopt to put a thorough end to this disorder. Whosoever there be in the king's realm who devote themselves to keeping cattle and the farm, to them let his majesty give food and seed corn. Whosoever there be in the king's realm who devote themselves to trade, to them let his majesty give capital. Whosoever there be in the king's realm who devote themselves to government service, to them let his majesty give wages and food. Then those men, following each his own business, will no longer harass the realm; the king's revenue will go up; the country will be quiet and at peace; and the populace pleased with one another and happy, dancing their children in their arms, will dwell with open doors.[48]

The above analysis recognizes that men and women can be pushed to violence if the prevailing conditions do not enable them to preserve their own lives without it. The instinct to survive is credited with enough strength to push people to struggle before they will sink into need. In such a situation, it follows that to press down the hand of the law will not be effective. In fact, it could encourage a growth in serious crime.

This is what happens in the Cakkavatti Sīhanāda Sutta, another mythological story dealing with disruption in society. It has already been mentioned with reference to the duty of kingship. But there is one clause concerning his duty that has not yet been mentioned: "Throughout your kingdom let no wrongdoing prevail. And whosoever in your kingdom is poor, to him let wealth be given."[49] The kings of the story who keep to this are blessed with peace. Yet a king eventually arises who neglects the giving of wealth to the poor. He is soon faced with a situation beyond his control. Poverty becomes rampant and this leads to theft, since people would rather steal than die. When the king realizes the cause, he starts by being lenient on the wrongdoer, by giving him the means to live. Such kindness too late leads others to see the only way to survive is turning to theft and receiving a royal handout in return. The king has given charity, not justice, and crime increases leading to a return to brutal punishments. The brutality of the punishments encourages the people to be more extreme in their own crime as they try to survive. Punishment here fails to deter because of the desperation of the people.

The sutta presents a disturbing picture of how a society can fall into utter confusion because of a lack of economic justice. The extremes reached are far greater than anything envisaged in the Kūṭadanta Sutta and they stem from the state's blindness to the realities of poverty. Thus the sutta states in refrain after every deterioration:

> Thus from goods not being bestowed on the destitute, poverty … stealing … violence … murder … lying … evil-speaking … immorality grew rife.

Theft and killing lead to false speech, jealousy, adultery, incest and perverted lust until:

> Among such humans, brethren, there will arise a sword-period (*satthantarakappa*) of seven days during which they will look on each other as wild beasts; sharp swords will appear ready to their hands, and they thinking, "This is a wild beast, this is a wild beast," will with their swords deprive each other of life.[50]

In the Cakkavatti Sīhanāda Sutta, the nourishment of the violence is the state's neglect of the poor. The whole myth illustrates the principle of *paṭicca samuppāda*. Each state of degeneration is dependent on the state before it. An evolutionary process is seen. An inevitability seems to emerge, an inevitable movement towards bestiality. It is significant that the sutta does not concentrate on the psychological state of the people. The obsessive cravings which overtake them are traced back to the failure of the state rather than to failings in their own adjustment to reality. The root is the defilement in the state—the *rāga, dosa* and *moha* in the king which afflict his perception of his duty.

An Aṅguttara Nikāya passage states this principle in simple and direct terms. If the king is righteous, his ministers will be righteous, the country will be righteous and the natural world will be a friend rather than an enemy. The opposite, of course, is also true and is placed first in the sutta:

> At such time, monks, as rulers are unrighteous (*adhammikā*), their ministers are unrighteous, brahmins and householders are also unrighteous....[51]

The above passages show that a change of heart is needed where violence exists but this change is needed in those who wield power in society. When a state is corrupt, the citizens become victims of the state and their own wish to survive and they are then led to actions they would never consider if they were free from want. There is an understanding that, besides those who do evil, there exists a category of people to whom wrong is done and whose reactions are conditioned by the original wrongdoing.

To pass now to the psychological roots of violence, another myth can be cited, the Aggañña Sutta. Like the Cakkavatti Sīhanāda Sutta, it describes an evolutionary process which takes on its own momentum. The root of the process is significant—the craving of beings. The sutta explains, in myth form, the process by which undifferentiated beings come to earth from a World of Radiance to eat the earth's savoury crust, to the point where there is private property and the division of labour. One of its purposes is to challenge the static, non-evolutionary theory of a divinely ordained caste system but it is significant also because evolution is guided by the growth of craving and individualism. The whole sutta turns on the individual and his craving as the root of violence. It depicts a situation before state power is established. Craving first enters when the beings taste the crust of the earth:

> Then, Vāseṭṭha, some being of greedy disposition said, "Lo now, what will this be?" and tasted the savoury earth with his finger. He thus, tasting, became suffused with the savour, and craving (taṇhā) entered into him.[52]

The craving develops. The natural world evolves to accommodate the beings, becoming ever less easy to manage. The bodies of the beings become gross and individually differentiated into male and female, comely and unlovely. Jealousy and competition enter. The savoury crust disappears. Vegetables and plant life evolve. An important point is reached when the beings establish boundaries around their individually owned rice plots. Individualism is therefore institutionally consolidated and the consequence is violence:

> Now some being, Vāseṭṭha, of greedy disposition, watching over his plot, stole another plot and made use of it. They took him and, holding him fast, said, "Truly, good being, you have done evil in that, while watching your own plot, you have stolen

another plot and made use of it. See, good being, that you do no such thing again." "Aye, sirs," he replied. And a second time he did so. And yet a third. And again they took him and admonished him. Some smote him with the hand, some with clods, some with sticks. With such a beginning, Vāseṭṭha, did stealing appear and censure and lying and punishment became known.[53]

The sutta illustrates that *taṇhā* coupled with individualism nourishes violence and conditions the necessity for state power to curb excesses. As such, its teaching is directly in the mainstream of Buddhist thought: craving and grasping lie at the root of negative and unwholesome states in society. However, more needs to be said about the causes and consequences of individualism.

The term "*puthujjana*" is used to describe the ordinary, average person:

> Herein, monks, an uninstructed ordinary person, taking no account of the pure ones (*ariyānaṁ*), unskilled in the Dhamma of the pure ones, untrained in the Dhamma of the pure ones, taking no account of the true men, unskilled in the Dhamma of the true men, untrained in the Dhamma of the true men, does not comprehend the things that should be wisely attended to, does not comprehend the things that should not be wisely attended to.[54]

The term "*puthu*" has two main meanings: "several, many, numerous," on one hand, and "separate, individual," on the other. The usual definition of *puthujjana* is "one of the many folk," linking it with the first of the above-mentioned meanings. However, a case can be made for the second meaning also. In this analysis, the *puthujjana* is one who believes himself to be separate from the rest of humankind; one who believes he has a self to be protected, promoted and pampered. It is this assumption which leads to so much that is disruptive in society.

Violent tendencies link, at this point, with the defilement of *moha* (delusion): delusion in terms of a misunderstanding of *anicca* and *anattā*. The latter states that there is no abiding, unchanging substance within the human being. Men and women are verbs rather than nouns, causal processes rather than unchanging souls. Buddhism does not deny that there is a person, but it reformulates the definition of what constitutes a person to embrace continuity rather than static entity. As the sound of the lute cannot be found within the lute as it is taken apart, so the "I am" cannot be found in the human personality when it is dissected into the five *khandhas*.[55]

Much anger and violence stem from the felt need to defend what is seen to be one's own or to grasp personal gain. It is a need which sees the gain of others as a threat to personal power and the rights of others as an attack on personal prestige. This is none other than the fault of the *puthujjana*, a failure to see the truth of *anattā* and the interdependence of all phenomena. It is this failure which leads to the self becoming the touchstone and measuring rule for every perception and judgement. It is the failure which leads to the urge to be violent in defence of needs and seeming rights. The Aggañña Sutta shows this ego illusion manifesting itself in the form of competitive individualism. That the ego illusion and *taṇhā* feed on one another is a theme found in many texts:

Monks, I will teach you the craving that ensnares, that floats along, that is far flung, that clings to one, by which this world is smothered, enveloped, tangled like a ball of thread, covered as with blight, twisted up like a grass rope, so that it does not pass beyond the Constant Round, the Downfall, the Way of Woe, the Ruin....

Monks, when there is the thought: "I am"—there come to be the thoughts: "I am in this world; I am thus; I am otherwise; I am not eternal; I am eternal; Should I be? Should I be in this world? Should I be thus? Should I be otherwise? May I become. May I become in this world. May I become thus. May

I become otherwise. I shall become. I shall become otherwise."
These are the eighteen thoughts which are haunted by craving
(*taṇhāvicaritāni*) concerning the inner self (*ajjhattikassa*).[56]

One result of this interdependent feeding, the Buddhist texts assert,
is disruption in society.

Another important area of study is the mechanism through which
the "I" notion helps to generate unwholesome states. Buddhism sees
a danger in the view of some schools of psychology that there is a
creative use of the concept of self. In this respect, the Pali term
"*papañca*," commonly translated as proliferation, is important. The
Madhupiṇḍika Sutta declares *papañca* to be the root of taking up
weapons, and the defeat of *papañca* is the way to end such violence:

> This is itself an end to the propensity to ignorance, this is it-
> self an end of taking a weapon, of quarrelling, contending, dis-
> puting, accusation, slander, lying speech.[57]

As the previous analysis in this paper points out, discrimination
is central to the Buddhist approach and therefore generalizations such
as the above need to be studied carefully. There is no doubt, however, that *papañca* is central to a Buddhist psychology of violence
and to an understanding of the danger in the "I am" notion.

A study by Bhikkhu Ñāṇananda, *Concept and Reality*, gives extensive coverage to the term "*papañca*".[58] He puts forward the view
that it is linked with the final stage of sense cognition and that it
signifies a "a spreading out, a proliferation" in the realm of concepts, a tendency for the conceptual process to run riot and obscure
the true reality of things. He makes much use of the above-quoted
Madhupiṇḍika Sutta and quotes the following:

> Visual consciousness, brethren, arises because of eye and vis-
> ible forms; the meeting of the three is sensory impingement;
> because of sensory impingement arises feeling (*vedanā*); what
> one feels, one perceives (*sañjānāti*); what one perceives, one

reasons about (*vitakketi*); what one reasons about, one turns into *papañca* (*papañceti*); what one turns into *papañca,* due to that *papañca-saññā-saṅkhā* assail him in regard to visible forms cognizable by the eye belonging to the past, the future and the present.[59]

The same is said of the other senses.

Ñāṇananda points out that a grammatical analysis of the above reveals that the process of perception involves deliberate activity up until *papañceti*. After this, deliberation vanishes. The subject becomes the object. The person who reasons conceptually becomes the victim of his own perceptions and thought constructions. So Ñāṇananda writes:

> Like the legendary resurrected tiger which devoured the magician who restored it to life out of its skeletal bones, the concepts and linguistic conventions overwhelm the worldling who evolved them. At the final and crucial stage of sense-perception, the concepts are, as it were, invested with an objective character.[60]

His analysis is of immense significance to the study of how certain negative and destructive tendencies can grow in society; how objective perception and reason can seem to fade before the force of what might be irrational and obsessive. He roots the cause in the nature of language in the minds of persons governed by *taṇhā, māna* and *diṭṭhi*—craving, conceit (the tendency to measure oneself against others), and views—which in themselves flow from ego-consciousness. *Papañca,* according to this analysis, manifests itself through *taṇhā, māna* and *diṭṭhi*. It underlies each of these qualities and breeds conflict in society.

To look at the process in more detail: The conventions of language enter near the beginning of the process of sense perception, at the point where feeling gives rise to mental activity and concepts. The mind, if unchecked, will attempt to place order on its feelings through language. This language immediately introduces the duality of subject and object, subject and feeling. The "I" enters with "I feel aversion" or "I feel attraction" or "I like this" or" I don't like this." This emphasis on the "I" is predetermined by the very nature of language and reinforces the strength of the feeling and the tendency for the person to identify completely with what is felt. What seems to happen after that is that language takes on a dynamism of its own. Concepts proliferate and leave the empirical behind, under the driving force of *taṇhā, māna* and *diṭṭhi*. For instance, the observation, "I feel aversion" might lead to further thoughts such as:

> I am right to feel aversion.... Therefore, the object is inherently worthy of aversion.... So, the object must threaten me and others.... Therefore the objects must be got rid of.... I cannot survive unless the object is annihilated from my sphere of vision and feeling.... It is my duty to annihilate this for my sake and the sake of others.

Thus the entrance of "I" leads to the urge to protect the wishes of the ego and what is ego-based becomes a seemingly rational decision about duty. The above is a purely hypothetical progression, yet it is not an implausible one. It illustrates the way in which thought progresses further and further away from what is empirically observed. Speculation enters as the mind attempts to reason. Eventually, as the thought process develops further, what might appear to be reason cloaks obsession which, in turn, can make the person a victim of the apparent logic of language.

Kant in his *Critique of Pure Reason*[61] seems to adopt a similar point of view. He challenged the view that speculative metaphysics using the categories of pure reason could extend our knowledge of reality. He attacked particularly those theologians who believed that the existence of God could be proved through logic alone. There was, he claimed, an irresistible impulse of the mind towards seeking unification and synthesis which led to the illegitimate use of language. It is this which is particularly relevant to this study. For instance, he posited that the mind assumed an unconditional personal ego just because all representations were unified by the "I think" construction. It also assumed a concept of God because of the drive to find an unconditioned unity. Such concepts, Kant felt, arose through the impulse of the mind and passed beyond the legitimate purview of language. It passed beyond the perceptions which could add knowledge and were not based on truly empirical data. Therefore, they could not give statements with any factual reality.

Kant grasped that there was an irresistible impulse which led to concepts taking on an unwarranted life of their own. Buddhism says that these concepts can generate obsessions, victimize the person who believes he or she is thinking logically, and lead to disruption in society. What is lost in the process is the ability to see objectively and value the empirical through senses unclouded by craving, conceit and views, or by greed, hatred and delusion.

Papañca, fed and generated by *taṇhā*, is therefore central to the theme of violence in the thoughts and actions of human beings. Buddhism suggests that the human person can become the victim of obsessive actions, thoughts and inclinations. It holds that the drift towards violence within one person or within society, especially if a communal or cultural obsession has arisen, may become an inevitable causal process unless the inner mechanism is discovered. Related to this is the danger and motivating force of dogmatic and speculative views as one of the roots of violence—the *diṭṭhi*, connected in the above analysis with *papañca*. In his advice to the Kālāmas and to Bhaddiya, the Buddha said:

> Be not mislead by report or tradition or hearsay. Be not misled by proficiency in the Collections, nor by mere logic or inference, nor after considering reasons, nor after reflection on or approval of some theory, nor because it fits becoming, nor by the thought: the recluse is revered by us.[62]

Here, logic and inference are deemed to be as dangerous as what is passed on by doubtful report and tradition. The same approach is seen in the Brahmajāla Sutta[63] where a number of mistaken views, according to Buddhist analysis, are discussed. *Taṇhā* is seen as the root of these but logic and inference are also mentioned.

In the following, the question of conflict in relation to dogmatic views is more clearly expressed. The Buddha points out the danger of saying, "This is indeed the truth, all else is falsehood" (*idam-eva saccaṁ, mogham-aññaṁ*). For dispute is the result and: "If there is dispute, there is contention; if there is contention, there is trouble; if there is trouble there is vexation."[64] Adhering dogmatically to views is a form of *papañca*, a particularly dangerous form. Several suttas in the Sutta Nipāta take up this theme: the Pasūra Sutta and the Kalahavivāda Sutta,[65] for instance. The former speaks of the person who goes forth roaring, looking for a rival to contest with, filled with pride and arrogance over his theories. A battle-like situation is implied, an attitude closely allied to that which actually results in warfare and armed struggle. Contemporary struggles in the world give ample evidence to prove that war and struggle are caused by the conflict of ideas, ideologies and concepts. They show how powerful and charismatic a force ideas can be. Whether it is nationalism, ethnicity or religion, groups can be pushed towards violence in defence of them. Buddhist analysis points out that some ideologies which might appear logical could, in fact, be the fruit of *papañca*. Adherents may be convinced of their truth but they might have progressed far from analysis based on empirical data.

In the above analysis of the roots of violence, two broad areas have been studied: the external and the internal, the environmental and psychological. Yet the two are not separate. They interconnect and feed one another, just as external sense objects interconnect with the senses, giving rise to consciousness and psychological processes. If a people's environment is unhealthy, corrupt or unjust, the seeds are sown for violent resistance, through the growth of motivating ideologies which take on a life of their own as they grip the minds of those who are being oppressed. If the environment is excessively competitive, consumer-oriented and materialistic, *taṇhā* will quickly arise, develop and expand into obsessive patterns of greed, taking over and dominating the perception of people who find themselves victims of craving rather than masters of their own perceptual processes. The step to violence is then small. If other elements are present, such as a group without access to the wealth visible in others, discrimination against minorities or racism, then the drive towards violence will be more rapid.

4

Can Violent Tendencies Be Eradicated?

There is an optimism at the heart of Buddhism. The Four Noble Truths and *paṭicca samuppāda* present a doctrine of hope because they affirm change and evolution. Men and women are not pawns of fate, chance or a capricious metaphysical being.[66] They can be makers of their own future. Applied to the issue of violence and disruption, this means that violence within the individual and in society is not intransigent, although the Buddhist texts make it quite clear that the obstacles to transformation are large.

Buddhism has no concept of a worldly utopia. *Saṃsāra* is *saṃsāra,* characterized by *dukkha*. *Nibbāna* is a victory over *saṃsāra*, not a destruction of *saṃsāra*. The doctrine of *anicca* (impermanence), in fact, undermines any dream of a golden future or a straight road of development towards harmony and peace. Yet the worth of working for conditions for concord is never denied. The important questions which emerge are: How feasible is the lessening of violent tendencies in society? Can changes in the individual affect society as a whole? When there is violence inherent in the structures of society, what steps can be taken?

To take the possibility for change within the individual first, certain passages from the texts suggest that the Buddha had rather a low opinion of the *puthujjana* and his or her ability to change. Verse 174 of the Dhammapada reads:

> Blind is the world
> Few are those who clearly see.
> As birds escape from a net
> Few go to a blissful state.

His sermons show that he recognizes that reaching people set on material things with a new message is difficult because their perception and ability to hear has been conditioned by the pattern of their craving:

> But this situation exists, Sunakkhatta, when some individual here may be set on the material things of this world (*lokā-misādhimutto*), and the talk of the individual who is set on the material things of this world follows a pattern in accordance with which he reflects and ponders, and he associates with that man under whom he finds felicity; but when there is talk about imperturbability (*ānañja*) he does not listen, does not lend an ear, does not rouse his mind to profound knowledge, and he does not associate with that man under whom he does not find felicity.[67]

> A bad man, monks, is possessed of bad states of mind, he consorts with bad men, he thinks as do bad men, he advises as do bad men, he speaks as do bad men, he acts as do bad men, he has the views of bad men, he gives gifts as do bad men.... And how, monks, does a bad man act as do bad men? As to this monks, a bad man is one to make onslaught on creatures, to take what has not been given, to enjoy himself wrongly...[68]

In one passage, a prince, Prince Jayasena, is pictured in conversation with a novice monk who speaks about aloofness and one-pointedness of mind. On the evidence given, the prince declares such an achievement to be impossible. Confused, the novice goes to the Buddha, who says that such direct teaching could not possibly have been understood by one of such a lifestyle as the prince:

> That Prince Jayasena, living as he does in the midst of sense pleasures, enjoying sense pleasures, being consumed by thoughts of sense pleasures, burning with the fever of sense pleasure, eager in the search of sense pleasures, should know or see or attain or realize that which can be known by renunciation, realized by renunciation—such a situation does not exist.[69]

The above passages might seem to imply the reverse of hope on the very same ground as hope was confirmed in the introduction to this section—*paṭicca samuppāda*. If perception is conditioned by a person's lifestyle, the friends he or she chooses, and greed for material objects, then appreciation of another set of values will not arise from that nourishment. Such an argument would seem to be realistic given the framework of conditionality. However, this realism must be balanced with instances in the texts where change does take place in the lives of individuals.

The case of Angulimāla is one of the best known and most frequently quoted. Angulimāla is a multiple murderer, the terror of Sāvatthī. He is described as having depopulated villages and districts through his urge to kill. The Angulimāla Sutta describes the story.[70] The Buddha, ignoring the fear of the people, sets out by himself toward where Angulimāla is said to be. Angulimāla, on seeing him, decides to give him the same fate as others who had dared to walk the roads. However, at this point, the Buddha uses a technique which slaps Angulimāla so hard that he gains sudden insight into the futility of the path he had been taking. The Buddha uses his psychic power to ensure that Angulimāla cannot catch up with him, however much effort he applies. This opens up the opportunity for the question of walking and standing still to be raised. Angulimāla is forced into the realization that his life has been a futile chase, a fretful searching, without peace or fulfilment. The tranquillity of the Buddha contrasts sharply with his own turbulence and the destructive state of his mind. The contrast makes him see the nature of his mind. A revolution—in its true sense of a complete turning around—takes place. Angulimāla, the murderer, becomes a completely changed person. He asks the Buddha for ordination as a monk, and soon becomes an Arahant, a saint.

Some interpretations have attempted to explain this in terms of a form of grace coming from the Buddha to the murderer. No doubt the person of the Buddha had a profound effect on the man. The sheer contrast between the states of mind and consequent physical appearance and bearing of the two would have shaped the event. Yet it is perhaps more helpful to think of Angulimāla as being ready to change, ready to face what he was doing to his life. The Buddha's words acted as a sudden jolt to shock him into realization and change. A similar transformation can be seen at the end of the Cakkavatti Sīhanāda Sutta, mentioned earlier, when bestiality has overtaken society to the point that a reaction takes place. At the point when beings think of one another as wild beasts, some begin to think:

> Let us not slay anyone; nor just let anyone slay us. Let us now, therefore, take ourselves to dens of grass, or dens in the jungle, or holes in trees, or river fastnesses, or mountain clefts and subsist on fruits and on roots of the jungle.[71]

The depth of barbarism causes a reversal, a disgust with the nourishment on which violent thoughts were feeding. Something new seems to enter but it is nevertheless part of the ongoing causal process. The important point is that there can be a stage at which the unwholesome is recognized as such by those who are perpetrating it. The process through which those who followed the Buddha saw the household life as a fetter, a state in which it was difficult to avoid greed, materialism and competitiveness, to a certain extent parallels this.[72]

That it is possible for people to change accords with human experience. It is also worth going back to the advice given to the novice who had tried to instruct Prince Jayasena.[73] The story does not end with the Buddha's words about the impossibility of reaching the mind of the prince. An alternative method is stressed—gradual training. The Buddha explains that the prince might have understood if told that the process of understanding was gradual. The simile of the training of an elephant is used: At first, the elephant is brought from the forest into the open; he is addressed with kindly words and fed; then tasks are given to him, progressing from the simple to the more complex up to the point where the animal can endure blows of the sword and the din of war without flinching.

The stress on a gradual process of change and training, beginning with moral habit, stretches like a thread across the Buddhist texts. There is a firm belief that discipline, education and the taking of one step at a time can lead people from a state of relative ignorance to greater wisdom. The possibility of gradual change must be admitted alongside the sudden change of Angulimāla. The two are complementary.

In the Kevaddha Sutta, Kevaddha, a young householder, comes to the Buddha and pleads with him to perform a mystic wonder.[74] The Buddha names three wonders of which he has knowledge: the mystic, the wonder of manifestation, and the wonder of education. The first two are to be feared and abhorred. It was the latter which was to be praised as the most worthy—the wonder of education. Change through a gradual process is, therefore, deemed possible but it is also recognized as something of a wonder, given the strength of craving and grasping.

Evidence that groups of both lay and ordained people were following the gradual training comes from the Mahāparinibbāna Sutta. The sutta speaks of the fourfold society being a reality—the fourfold society as composed of monks, nuns, laymen and laywomen. Māra is seen to approach the Buddha, urging him to die because the task he had set himself earlier had been completed:

> Now is the time for the Exalted One to pass away—even according to the word which the Exalted One spoke when he said, "I shall not die, O Evil One, until the brethren and the sisters of the Order and until the lay disciples of both sex shall have become true hearers, wise and well-trained, ready and learned, carrying the doctrine in their memory, masters of the lesser corollaries that follow from the larger doctrine, correct in life, walking according to the precepts—until they, having thus themselves learnt the doctrine, shall be able to tell others of it, preach it, make it known, establish it, open it, minutely explain it and make it clear."[75]

In the above description, both lay and ordained are described with the same adjectives. Lay people as well as ordained are credited with considerable knowledge. There are grounds of hope here, since the first stage of gradual training is morality, the foundation of which is the Five Precepts. All of these are linked with abstaining from different forms of violence: direct and indirect killing; theft; the exploitation of women; the violence connected with speech; violence to oneself through the use of drugs. The Early Buddhist texts are replete with exhortations to keep the precepts. Heaven and hell, bliss and torture, are held up and paeons of praise are given to those who follow them:

> Faint is the fragrance of *tagara* and sandal
> But the fragrance of the virtuous is excellent
> Wafting even among the gods.

Dhp. v. 56.

There are examples, however, of lay people going beyond morality. Pessa, the son of an elephant trainer, claims:

> And, revered sir, we householders too, dressed in white, from time to time dwell with our minds well applied to the four applications of mindfulness (*catusu satipaṭṭhānesu*).[76]

Pessa receives the recognition and praise of the Buddha for this. It is significant that mindfulness is crucial in halting the flow of mind, in halting *papañca,* as described earlier, and the violent thoughts which might consequently flow. The key to mindfulness is the development of the ability to stand aside, detached from what is happening to the body, to feeling, to thought processes and mental objects,[77] so that ever arising and passing movement, feelings and thoughts are carefully charted. It is an approach which recognizes both *anicca* and *anattā: anicca* because what is attended to is seen as an ever-changing process; *anattā,* because the elements of the process are not assumed to belong to the person and therefore are not clung to as unchanging truths. Mindfulness (*satipaṭṭhāna*) in fact can stop the mind before obsessions based on *taṇhā*, *māna* and *diṭṭhi* can grow.

Guarding the doors of the senses (*indriya saṁvara*) is one form of practice of mindfulness, frequently mentioned as the second step in the gradual training. The traditional way of describing this is:

> Having seen a visible form with the eye, he is not entranced by the general appearance, he is not entranced by the detail. If he dwells with his organ of sight uncontrolled, covetousness and dejection, evil unskilled states of mind, might predominate. So he fares along controlling it, he guards the organ of sight, he achieves control over the organ of sight.[78]

The same is said of the other sense organs. A guard is placed at the point where contact between the sense and the sense object results in feeling (*vedanā*). Knowledge of how the mind works is gained. Mindfulness is thus an antidote to *papañca* and stops the mechanism through which *papañca* develops. It demands effort and discipline. The texts show that such mind-culture is possible and suggest that it would lead to the lessening of violence as an expression of personal greed.

The example of the Sangha, the Order of Monks, must also be looked at. No compromises were made concerning violence when it came to the monk. The Sangha was intended to be a model of harmonious interpersonal relationships. It was to provide an alternative set of values to lay people, to present a pattern of sharing rather than of competitive individualism.[79] If the Sangha had been able to carry out succesfully this role, a disturbing challenge would have been presented to the communities among which the monks walked.

The Kakacūpama Sutta is one of the best examples of the extent to which violent retaliation was condemned for the monk. The key sentence, repeated many times, speaks of the attitude to be cultivated in the face of abuse or violence:

Neither will my mind become perverted, nor will I utter evil speech, but kindly and compassionate will I dwell with a mind of friendliness and devoid of hatred (*mettacitto no dosantaro*).

What is significant is the extent to which this is to be taken:

Monks, as low-down thieves might carve one limb from limb with a double-handed saw, yet even then whoever sets his mind at enmity, he, for this reason, is not a doer of my teaching. Herein, monks, you must train yourself: Neither will our minds become perverted ... devoid of hatred.[80]

The Puṇṇovāda Sutta describes a monk who took this teaching to heart. He intends to travel to a district where the people are known to be hostile. The Buddha questions him about how he will deal with abuse and violence. Possibilities are mentioned, increasing each time in intensity from verbal abuse to loss of life. After each one, Puṇṇa responds by saying that he would be thankful that the abuse was not even more serious. When the Buddha finally mentions murder, he says:

If the people of Sunāparanta deprive me of life with a sharp knife, revered sir, it will be thus for me there; I will say, "There are disciples of the Lord who, disgusted by the body and the life-principle and ashamed of them, look about for a knife. I have come to this knife without having looked for it."[81]

He is said to have made a thousand followers, suggesting that his attitude became a true inspiration to a people who were characterized by violence.

In contrast to the above, there are examples of monks presenting a harmful example to lay people. As the Sangha grew in number and in reputation, the initial enthusiasm of the first disciples became diffused. Evidence in suttas such as the Bhaddāli Sutta, the Kākacūpama Sutta, the Kīṭāgiri Sutta and the Anumāna Sutta[82] shows that there were forces of deterioration. Some monks were difficult to exhort; some were rebellious towards the rules; some were incapable of taking correction from others. In this way, their ability to provide an example to lay people would have been weakened. Yet it would be wrong to place too much emphasis on this weakness. Other suttas can be quoted to show what an impact the Buddha's followers had on other groups of wanderers and even on kings.[83]

The important point here is that hope for change in the Early Buddhist texts also lies in the Sangha as example and educator. Lay people were encouraged to show devotion to the Sangha and to listen to its teaching. As outlined above, there is evidence that there was a body of lay people who were very serious in their striving to undertake the precepts and to train their mind so that *tanhā* could be reduced. That change in the individual is possible is confirmed by a study of the early followers.

The above picture combines hope with realism. The obstacles mentioned at the beginning of the section must not be overlooked; the barriers to change are great. According to Buddhism the average person (*puthujjana*) will often need the threat of punishment, either in the present or in a future life, to be deterred from socially disruptive activities. It has also been pointed out that it is not enough to concentrate on the individual. A society is more than the sum of its individuals. Just as the human person is such because of the specific relationship between the five *khandhas,* so a society takes on its character because of the way in which its parts are organized through institutions, traditions and external influences.

The next question which must be looked at is how the individual can affect society as a whole or, more exactly, what the consequences are when a person follows the gradual training of Buddhism. As with the other questions raised, the method of this paper is to discover what the texts say, to uncover the guidelines or resources they provide for the analysis of contemporary issues.

In a previous section it was suggested that one of the causes of violence was the proliferation of concepts and ideas flowing from the perceptual process when governed by *taṇhā, māna* and *diṭṭhi.* Is the answer, then, a retreat into silence and inaction away from all concepts? The evidence suggests not. The Buddha was quick to condemn any inference that he taught a doctrine of either inaction or apathy. One example will illustrate this. The Buddha is seen in conversation with a person called Potaliya. Potaliya declares that the most worthy person is the one who speaks neither in dispraise of what deserves not praise nor in praise of the praiseworthy. He advocates what would seem a complete withdrawal from judgement and a supreme detachment from the issues governing society. And the term Potaliya uses to describe the frame of mind he is talking about is *upekkhā*—equanimity.

The Buddha, however, disagrees with him. Far better is the person of discrimination who speaks in dispraise of the unworthy and in praise of the praiseworthy, saying seasonably what is factual and the truth. In other words, he challenges the view that *upekkhā* (equanimity) means the quality Potaliya advocates. The Buddha puts forward another quality:

> Now, Potaliya, there are these four persons existing in the world.... Of these four persons, Potaliya, he who speaks in dispraise of what deserves not praise and in praise of the praiseworthy, saying seasonably what is fact and true—he is the most admirable and rare. Why so? Because, Potaliya, his discrimination of proper occasions (*kālaññutā*) is admirable.[84]

The Buddha mentions the quality of *kālaññutā,* in place of the word used by Potaliya—*upekkhā.* The translation given by the Pali Text Society is "discrimination of proper occasions." The ability to discriminate and make objective evaluations, not indifference, is the consequence of curbing *papañca.* A certain silence of the mind is indicated but it is not the silence of apathy. The proliferation of concepts which is *papañca* results in an obscuring of the empirical, since this proliferation moves one further and further away from the empirical because of the linguistic edifice of "therefore" and "therein" erected on top of the initial emotion of like or aversion. Preventing the erection of this edifice on the foundation of *taṇhā* leads to a clearer perception of the empirical and to judgements and analyses being made with greater validity. The conclusions reached through *papañca* may seem to be analytical. They are not. Resisting *papañca* is not a moving away from analysis but a moving towards objective analysis unclouded by emotional responses. It is this kind of analysis which is so often lacking when there is violence and conflict in society.

When perceptions, judgements and consequent action are governed by the roots of *papañca*, there will be no objectivity but a danger that obsessions will grow. When *papañca* is allayed, what is good and bad, *kusala* and *akusala*, praiseworthy and blameworthy, will be more clearly visible. The injustices in society, for instance, will be more apparent. Judgements about those who are oppressed in society or about those who gain wealth illegally through violence and extortion will not be clouded either by the tendency to look down on those who suffer or the wish to gain patronage from the wealthy. What is wrong and what is right, what harms and what promotes happiness, will stand out untouched by personal wishes or personal greed.

This clarity of judgement can be seen in the words of the Buddha. In the Assalāyana Sutta, the Aggañña Sutta and the Madhura Sutta the caste system is vigorously opposed.[85] The Esukārī Sutta condemns the kind of service which becomes slavery.[86] Meaningless ritual is attacked in the Sigālovāda Sutta.[87] Brahminical excesses are uncovered in the Brahmajāla Sutta, the Ambaṭṭha Sutta and the Tevijja Sutta.[88] The violence and shame of sacrifices is condemned in the Kūṭadanta Sutta.[89] These are not the only examples. The Buddha is revealed as a person who was unafraid to point out wrong when he saw it and to use uncompromising words. It is this kind of effective speech and action which should flow when *taṇhā*, *māna* and *diṭṭhi* are reduced.

Abstention from the harmful or violent is not enough by itself.

The texts stress that the active cultivation of the opposite is necessary. A replacement is needed as well as an annihilation. This is seen at lay level as well as among the ordained. For instance, in the Sāleyyaka Sutta, addressed specifically to lay people, the two courses of faring by Dhamma and not-Dhamma are explained. Malevolence is explained by reference to the wish to kill:

> He is malevolent in mind, corrupt in thought and purpose, and thinks: "Let these beings be killed or slaughtered or annihilated or destroyed or may they not exist at all."[90]

Faring by Dhamma is explained in opposite terms and yet the effect is not merely a negation of or a restraining from not-Dhamma but the practice of positive virtue. So, the one who abandons slanderous speech becomes "a reconciler of those who are at variance and one who combines those who are friends." The one who restrains himself from malevolent thought is the one who thinks: "Let those beings, friendly, peaceful, secure, happy, look after self."[91] Similarly, during meditation, positive qualities are to be cultivated to replace the five hindrances. For instance:

> Putting away ill-will and hatred (*vyāpādapadosa*), he abides with heart free from enmity (*avyāpannacitta*), benevolent and compassionate towards every living being (*sabbe pānabhūta-hitānukampī*) and purifies his mind of malevolence.[92]

The Early Buddhist emphasis, therefore, indicates that the eradication of the tendencies which cause violence leads to greater realism, the growth of positive, wholesome qualities and more effective speech and action against what is unjust and exploitative. An important question, however, remains unanswered, the third question mentioned at the beginning of this section: When there is violence inherent in the structures of society as a whole, what steps can be taken?

In many societies, violence is institutionalized in structures which oppress certain sections of the people. Some would mention the caste system in India in this context, corrupt trading practices, or the forces which keep some groups of people poor. On the other hand, violence can flow from the monarchy or state, from internal terrorist groups or an outside threat. In these situations, violence is rarely lessened by changes in a few individuals, unless these individuals have considerable power. What strategies should be used to oppose such violence? Is there any situation where violence should be met with violence? Is there a different path for the lay person than for the monk? Is there a situation where it might be justifiable to overthrow the state? If so, could this lead to a changed society? If undeserved suffering occurs because of the greed of others, do the demands of compassion (*karuṇā*) ever involve what could be called violent resistance to the perpetrators? These are crucial questions in the light of current world tensions such as racial injustice, capitalistic monopolies, terrorism and fascism. The question here is whether any guidelines can be gained from the Buddhist texts themselves.

There is no doubt that the person who renounces the household life is called to abstain from violence completely. It is one of the hallmarks of the bhikkhu. Not to react in violent retaliation to abuse was part of the training of the disciple. Where there was state-instigated violence, the Early Buddhist position seems to have been that the Sangha could act as advisers to rulers and, in this capacity, could raise issues connected with righteous government, but it could not become involved in violent resistance. As for the lay follower of the Buddha, he or she undertakes to desist from harming others through the first precept. To break this intentionally is to risk serious kammic consequences. For the lay person, as for the monk, the approved line of action would seem to be advice and non-violent pressure or resistance towards those in a position to change violent structures.

A different set of responsibilities, however, is laid on the state itself. As previously discussed, rulers with the protection of their citizens at heart were inevitably drawn into conflict when threatened by aggression. The question can therefore be raised as to whether non-violence is an absolute value in Buddhism. For instance, is a father, as head and protector of the family, justified in using violence against a person forcefully entering his house with the intention to kill? Has an elder sister the duty to protect a younger brother if he is attacked violently, by using similar violence? Has a group of citizens the right to kill a dictator if, by doing so, they might save the lives of oppressed minorities to whom the citizens feel a duty? Should the terrorist gun be challenged with similar methods? These are areas where absolutes seem to break down. As a ruler might realize that some aggressor cannot be deterred by persuasion, so some citizens might feel that violence or injustice in society cannot be stopped merely by giving advice to those in power. That lay people should never initiate violence where there is harmony or use it against the innocent is very clear. That they should not attempt to protect those under their care if the only way of doing so is to use defensive violence is not so clear.

Guidelines about the consequences of violence, however, are laid down. The danger of violence, even if it is defensive, is that it will generate further violence. Non-hatred (*avera*) and loving kindness are the powers which halt it. *Mettā* (loving kindness) is shown to have great power: it can turn away the poison of a snake or the charge of an elephant;[93] it can render burning ghee harmless.[94] The latter story concerns a wife, Uttarā, who is married to an unbeliever. A courtesan, Sirimā, is given to her husband so that Uttarā can be released to attend on religious duties. A quarrel arises between the two women which ends in Sirimā pouring boiling ghee over Uttarā. As she prepares to do this, Uttarā thinks: "My companion has done me a favour. The circle of the earth is too narrow, the world of the devas is too low, but the virtue of my compassion is great because by her help, I have become able to give alms and listen to Dhamma. If I am angry with her may this ghee burn me; if not, let it not burn me." The ghee does not burn. Sirimā tries again. Then the other women present attack Sirimā and throw her to the ground. Uttarā continues to show compassion by coming to her rescue, by preventing her from being hurt.

Responding to violence with *mettā* and non-anger is deemed superior to any other path. Non-violent resistance is clearly the best path. Yet Buddhism cannot claim to be completely pacifistic. Absolutes of that kind cannot be found and perhaps should not be sought for in a teaching which spoke of the danger of claiming of a view, "this alone is truth, all else is falsehood." The person who feels violence is justified to protect the lives of others has indeed to take the consequences into account. He has to remember that he is risking grave consequences for himself in that his actions will inevitably bear fruit. He or she has to be aware that there is a dynamism within hatred and violence when the causal chain has not had its nourishment removed. Such a person needs to evaluate motives in the knowledge that violent tendencies are rooted in the defilements of *lobha*, *dosa* and *moha*, and in the obsessions generated by *papañca*. Yet that person might still judge that the risks are worth facing to prevent a greater evil. Whether the assassination of Hitler would have prevented numerous innocent deaths is still an open question.

In conclusion, it can be said that Buddhism lays down a form of mental culture to lessen the mind's tendency to veer towards violence. However, it is a culture which involves qualities of faith (*saddhā*) and effort (*vāyāma*) that many in society are unable to cultivate. Therefore punishment either by the state or in an afterlife is seen as a valid deterrent for extremes of violence. However, where violence flows directly and unjustifiably from the state or from other groups or institutions, questions are raised which are not dealt with directly by the texts. The drawing of conclusions is therefore fraught with difficulty. Yet these questions must be tackled if Buddhism is to provide guidelines in a violent world. What seems to emerge from the above analysis is that non-violence in the face of violence, although preferable for all and incumbent on the monk, is not a moral absolute in all circumstances.

Conclusion

It was claimed at the beginning that the advent of the nuclear bomb had issued in a new era of violence and that Buddhism should be able to address this development. The foregoing analysis started from a study of the Buddha's awareness of violence in his own society and passed to questions concerning the condemnation of violence, the roots of violence, and the possibilities for its eradication or reduction. Each of these issues has relevance for the present age, although it has been pointed out that many conditions have changed between the sixth century B.C. and the twentieth century A.D.

One area in which difference can be seen is in the nature of warfare. In the Buddha's time, professional armies were used to settle conflicts. Although civilians were no doubt killed as victorious armies took their plunder, it was the army itself which bore the brunt of the slaughter. Today the cost in civilian, animal and plant life in any future nuclear war is thinkable only in terms of the most horrific nightmare. The duty of the Cakkavatti King might be to defend his people. Yet no nuclear weapon can be used in defence. If it was, it would prove the Buddhist view that the use of violence leads to escalation. The slim, ever-shakey defence that nuclear weapons provide is MAD—Mutually Assured Destruction—an uneasy, computer-controlled peace feeding on fear and the willingness to annihilate millions in retaliation, if the other side dares to be the aggressor.

It would seem that, in nuclear weapons, man has created something out of his greed which now makes him victim. The analysis given earlier about the effects of *papañca* and the process of perception is relevant here. Some people might see the development of ever more sophisticated weapons of destruction as the result of objective, scientific probing into the nature of reality, in this case the use of the atom. An approach more in accordance with Buddhism would be to see the root as *tanhā*, *māna* and *ditthi*: the craving for power over the material world and over other people; the wish to protect self and judge other groups as inferior; the clinging to one ideology whilst condemning all others. The result of *tanhā*, *māna* and *ditthi* is *papañca*, the proliferation of ideas which turn the so-called perceiver into the victim of obsessions bearing little relation to the empirical. Nuclear and chemical weapons are horrific projections of the human mind. It has come to the point where they possess the mind rather than the mind the weapons. Humanity is now the victim.

Within this atmosphere, one may ask how effective change in the individual is and whether the few who work to conquer *tanhā*, *māna* and *ditthi* can act as leaven within the whole. The obstacles are great today as they were in the Buddha's time. The Buddha saw the *puthujjana* as a person hard to convince or change, given the strength of craving and views. Today, ideas have a charismatic force. Nationalism, ethnicity and religion, for instance, push groups towards violence. They form ego-feeding, identity-creating creeds which are hard to break down. In such situations, empirical evidence shows that some who try to show the alternative force of *mettā* become the victims of violence, at least in the frame of their present life.

Two insights from the foregoing study are relevant here: the reaction which took place in the Cakkavatti Sīhanāda Sutta and the interdependent nature of the environmental and the psychological. In the Cakkavatti Sīhanāda Sutta, the truth that violence leads to greater violence and crime to ever-deepening bestiality eventually pierces the consciousness of some members of society as they see what is happening around them. Some realize that change is possible through a change in thought patterns. A reaction takes place after the trough of bestiality has been reached. Today, there are those who are "turning around," who are realizing how destructive and bestial is the present and potential violence in the world. However, for just as long as the external environment remains tension-creating, the rise of violent tendencies will continue. Similar injustices exist today as are mentioned in the Kūṭadanta Sutta, but their scope has altered and widened to include relationships between blocks of countries as well as within countries. In most countries of the world, the poor are becoming poorer. Between countries, the richer nations are becoming richer at the expense of the poorer. The warning which the Buddhist texts give is that such conditions breed violence and that the arm of the law or the gun will not curb it. Only change at the level of the root causes will create more peaceful conditions. This is one of the gravest challenges which the world faces, since it points to a complete re-drawing of the world economic system. The formidable obstacle in the way of such change is *taṇhā* in those with power or economic might—for profit, influence and a luxurious lifestyle.

One reaction of the individual to the above tension is complete withdrawal into a life of inaction. This was evidently a temptation in the sixth century B.C. It has been a temptation across all religions throughout the centuries. The mistake is to confuse renunciation and inaction, detachment (*virāga*) and apathy. The life of renunciation aims at detachment from *rāga*, *dosa* and *moha*, but the result should not be apathy but rather greater compassion (*karuṇā*) and loving kindness (*mettā*). In the Samaṇamaṇḍikā Sutta, a wanderer, Uggāhamāna, declares that the one who does no evil deed with his body, speaks no evil speech, intends no evil intention and leads no evil livelihood is the recluse who has obtained the most worthy end. The Buddha responds:

> This being so carpenter, then according to the speech of Uggāhamāna a young baby boy lying on its back would be of abounding skill, of the highest skill, an unconquerable recluse, attained to the highest attainments.[95]

In contrast, the Buddha lays down the importance of developing wholesome qualities, not merely abstaining from what is unwholesome. The demands of the Eightfold Path are stressed, demands incumbent not only on the monk but on all followers:

> As to this, carpenter, a monk is endowed with the perfect view of an adept, he is endowed with the perfect intention of an adept, ... the perfect speech ... the perfect action ... the perfect mode of livelihood ... the perfect endeavour ... the perfect mindfulness ... the perfect concentration ... the perfect knowledge of an adept (*sammāñāṇena*), he is endowed with the perfect freedom of an adept.[96]

In a violent world, therefore, the duty of the Buddhist disciple is not inactive withdrawal or apathy but culture of the mind to root out personal defilements so that perception and judgement can be unbiased and objective; cultivation of positive qualities which will create harmony and peace; and, most important, a readiness to speak out and act against what is blameworthy and in praise of what is worthy of praise.

Notes

Abbreviations

DN	Dīgha Nikāya
MN	Majjhima Nikāya
SN	Saṁyutta Nikāya
AN	Aṅguttara Nikāya
Dhp	Dhammapada
Snp	Sutta Nipāta

Textual references have been taken from the Pali Text Society's editions of the Nikāyas. Unless specified otherwise, English translations have been taken from the PTS versions, though some have been slightly altered.

1. Utilitarianism is a philosophy which claims that the ultimate end of action should be the creation of human happiness. Actions should be judged according to whether they promote the greatest happiness of the greatest number. The most important exponent of this philosophy was the nineteenth century British thinker John Stuart Mill. One of the weaknesses of utilitarianism is that it can be used to justify the violation of minority rights.

2. Reference may be made to many texts which stress that encouraging others to do harm is blameworthy. AN ii,215, for instance, speaks of the unworthy man and the more unworthy man, the latter being one who encourages others to do harmful actions such as killing living beings.

3. MN 95/ii,167.

4. The Kosala Saṁyutta (Saṁyutta Nikāya, vol. 1) records the conversations which this king had with the Buddha. The examples mentioned have been taken from this section.

5.   SN i,97.

6.   MN 13/i,86-87.

7.   MN 13/i,87.

8.   SN iv,343.

9.   In several suttas, the Buddha comes across groups of wanderers engaged in heated discussions about kings, robbers, armies, etc. (e.g. DN iii,37; MN ii,1). In contrast, the Buddha advised his disciples either to maintain noble silence or to speak about the Dhamma.

10.   See Romila Thapar, *A History of India* (Pelican Books UK, 1966), chapter 3.

11.   SN i,75.

12.   MN 36/i,227ff.

13.   MN 12/i,68ff.

14.   At the end of the Buddha's description of his austerities in the Mahāsaccaka Sutta he says: "And some recluses and brahmins are now experiencing feelings that are acute, painful, sharp, severe; but this is paramount, nor is there worse than this. But I, by this severe austerity, do not reach states of further men, the excellent knowledge and vision befitting the Ariyans. Could there be another way to awakening?" (MN i,246).

15.   The Mahāsakuludāyi Sutta (MN 77/ii,1ff.) reflects contemporary realities when a town plays hosts to various groups of wanderers.

16.   DN 25/iii,38.

17.   DN 8/i,162.

18.   Trevor Ling, *The Buddha—Buddhist Civilisation in India and Ceylon* (Penquin Books UK, 1973).

19.   See Esukārī Sutta, MN 96.

20.   SN iv,330ff.

21.   DN 31.

22.   Reference can be made to the following:

  (a) AN i,188ff. The Buddha's advice to the Kālāmas.

  (b) AN ii,167ff. The Buddha advises the monks to scrutinize closely anything said to have come from his mouth.

(c) Cankī Sutta: MN 95/ii,170-71. The Buddha says that belief, reasoning and personal preference are not guarantees of truth.

(d) Vīmaṁsaka Sutta: MN 47. The Buddha urges his disciples to examine his own conduct before deciding whether he is an Enlightened One, and to investigate empirical evidence rather than accept things through blind faith.

23. The following texts provide fuller discussions about *paṭicca samuppāda*:

  (a) Sammādiṭṭhi Sutta: MN 9.
  (b) Mahātaṇhāsaṅkhaya Sutta: MN 38.
  (c) Mahānidāna Sutta: DN 15.

24. MN 99/ii,197.

25. MN 96/ii,177ff.

26. AN ii,42.

27. Reference may be made to the following:

  (a) Assalāyana Sutta: MN 93.
  (b) Madhura Sutta: MN 84.
  (c) AN ii,84. Here, four types of people are mentioned, two of whom are bound for light and two of whom are bound for darkness. Deeds, not birth, is the criterion for the divisions between the two sets.

28. For instance, the Kūṭadanta Sutta and the Cakkavatti Sīhanāda Sutta, to be discussed below.

29. The Mahādukkhakkhandha Sutta (MN 13) is an example.

30. SN i,100ff.

31. Therīgāthā vv. 105-6 (Soṇā).

32. MN 61/i,415-16.

33. MN 8/i,44-45.

34. AN ii,191.

35. *Mettā* and *karuṇā*, as two of the *brahmavihāras*, are mentioned at DN i,250-51, MN i,38, etc.

36. AN i,51.

37. MN 135/iii,303.

38.   MN 129/iii,169-70. A similar approach is adopted in the Devadūta Sutta: MN 130/iii,178ff.

39.   The Petavatthu is one of the books of the Khuddaka Nikāya. It contains 51 stories in four chapters, all concerning the *petas*, a class of ghost-like beings who have fallen from the human plane because of misdeeds done.

40.   DN 26/iii,61.

41.   DN 16/iii,72ff.

42.   SN i,82.

43.   SN i,83.

44.   SN i,101.

45.   SN iv,308.

46.   AN ii,121ff.

47.   Snp. vv. 935-38. Translation by H. Saddhatissa (Curzon Press, 1985).

48.   DN 5/i,135.

49.   DN 26/iii,61.

50.   DN iii,73.

51.   AN ii,74.

52.   DN 27/iii,85.

53.   DN iii,92.

54.   MN 2/i,7. The description of the *puthujjana* is a stock passage recurring throughout the Canon.

55.   See SN iv,195.

56.   AN ii,211.

57.   MN 18/i,109-10.

58.   Bhikkhu Ñāṇananda, *Concept and Reality in Early Buddhist Thought* (Kandy: Buddhist Publication Society, 1971).

59.   MN 18/i,111-12.

60.   *Concept and Reality*, p.6.

61.   Immanuel Kant, 1724-1804. His major work, *The Critique of Pure Reason*, studies the place of *a priori* ideas in the formation of concepts and examines the role of reason and speculative metaphysics.

62. AN i,188; AN ii,190.

63. DN 1. See e.g. DN i,16: "In the fourth case, monks, some recluse or brahmin is addicted to logic and reasoning. He gives utterance to the following conclusion of his own, beaten out by his argumentations and based on his sophistry...."

64. MN 74/i,497.

65. Snp. 824-34; Snp. 862-77.

66. AN ii,173ff. The Buddha here quotes three views which result in inaction: (i) that all feelings are due to previous kamma; (ii) that all feelings are due to a supreme deity; and (iii) that all feelings are without cause or condition.

67. MN 105/ii,253.

68. MN 110/iii,21-22.

69. MN 125/iii,129-30.

70. MN 86/ii,98ff.

71. DN 26/iii,73.

72. A stock passage found in many suttas (e.g. MN 51/i,344) extols the homeless life as the only way "to fare the holy life completely fulfilled, completely purified, polished like a conch shell."

73. Dantabhūmi Sutta: MN 125/iii,128ff.

74. DN 11/i,211.

75. DN 16/ii,104.

76. MN 51/i,340.

77. Body, feelings, thoughts and mental objects are the four foundations of mindfulness (see DN 22, MN 10).

78. MN 27/i,181, and elsewhere.

79. This point is developed in Trevor Ling, *The Buddha*.

80. MN 21/i,129.

81. MN 145/iii,269.

82. Respectively MN 65, MN 21, MN 70, MN 15.

83. The Mahāsakuludāyī Sutta (MN 77) and the Dhammacetiya Sutta

(MN 89) describe the impact which the general concord of the Buddha's followers had respectively on groups of wanderers at Rājagaha and on King Pasenadi.

84.   AN ii,100.

85.   Respectively MN 93, DN 27, MN 84.

86.   MN 96.

87.   DN 31/iii,181.

88.   Respectively DN 1, DN 3, DN 11.

89.   DN 5.

90.   MN 41/i,287.

91.   MN 41/i,288.

92.   DN 2/i,71 and elsewhere.

93.   See AN ii,71. A monk dies of snakebite, and the Buddha declares that if he had suffused the four royal families of snakes with a heart of *mettā*, he would not have died. A story in the Cullavagga of the Vinaya Piṭaka relates how the Buddha's envious cousin, Devadatta, tried to kill him by releasing a notoriously ferocious elephant called Nālāgiri at him in the streets of Rājagaha. The Buddha is said to have subdued it by exercising *mettā* and *karuṇā,* so that the elephant lowered its trunk and stopped before the Buddha. Hiuen-Tsang refers to a stupa at the place where this is said to have happened.

94.   Vimānavatthu, No. 15.

95.   MN 78/ii,24.

96.   MN 78/ii,29.

Concept and Reality in Early Buddhist Thought

Bhikkhu Ñāṇananda

This is an important original work of Buddhist philosophy, dealing with the problem of what the author calls "conceptual proliferation" (*papañca*), the mind's tendency to distort reality through its own conceptual activity. Building upon a suggestive passage in the famous Madhupindika Sutta, the author develops a thesis which ties together many important but seldom explored strands in early Buddhist thought. The book contains profoundly illuminating remarks on obscure passages from the Pali Canon, and has significant implications for philosophy, psychology and ethics.

Softback: 170 pages   135 mm x 210 mm
U.S. $6.00; SL Rs. 50   BP 404S

THE BUDDHIST PUBLICATION SOCIETY

The BPS is an approved charity dedicated to making known the Teaching of the Buddha, which has a vital message for people of all creeds. Founded in 1958, the BPS has published a wide variety of books and booklets covering a great range of topics. Its publications include accurate annotated translations of the Buddha's discourses, standard reference works, as well as original contemporary expositions of Buddhist thought and practice. These works present Buddhism as it truly is—a dynamic force which has influenced receptive minds for the past 2500 years and is still as relevant today as it was when it first arose. A full list of our publications will be sent upon request with an enclosure of U.S. $1.50 or its equivalent to cover air mail postage. Write to:

The Hony. Secretary
BUDDHIST PUBLICATION SOCIETY
P.O. Box 61
54, Sangharaja Mawatha
Kandy   Sri Lanka